# Sex

AND THE

# Family

IN THE

# Jewish

# Tradition

by
ROBERT GORDIS

THE BURNING BUSH PRESS
NEW YORK

To our daughters-in-love
Lucy, Dassy and Felice

*This volume is one of a series of popular presentations of basic aspects of Jewish life and thought, representative of views held within the Conservative Movement. Prepared under the auspices of the National Academy for Adult Jewish Studies of the United Synagogue of America, its publication has been made possible through the cooperation of the National Women's League of the United Synagogue.*

# Contents

# Foreword

The scholarly, yet popular, literature dealing with Judaism has been greatly enriched during the past two decades. Works on Jewish history, philosophy and liturgy as well as Biblical and Rabbinic subjects have become easily available to the English-reading public. Nonetheless, a number of areas of fundamental importance have not yet received their proper attention and due.

One such area is the concept of the family, its role and function within the Jewish tradition. While the general press is filled with chronicles of population explosion, divorce, birth control, revolutions in morality, and related matters, relatively little has been available which draws authentically on the rich resources of Jewish tradition in these matters of basic interest.

The National Academy is most pleased, therefore, to sponsor this contribution to a fuller understanding of sex and the family in the Jewish tradition. In it, Dr. Robert Gordis brings to bear the fruits of his creative scholarship as Seminary Professor of Bible at the Jewish Theological Seminary of America and an abiding concern with human problems sharpened by over three decades in the congregational rabbinate. Rabbi Gordis has earned a distinguished record for his contributions via the written and spoken word. The National Academy, sponsor of several of Dr. Gordis' earlier works, is pleased to present the current volume as a sorely-needed contribution to issues of paramount significance today. The Jewish tradition, with its profound insights, has much to offer all those — both Jews and non-Jews — concerned with the individual, the family and society itself.

We are happy to acknowledge the cooperation of the National Women's League of the United Synagogue of America in making this publication possible. This volume had its origin in an address delivered at the 1966 Biennial Convention of the Women's League. The expanded and revised text, accompanied by full documentation of sources and bibliography, is now made available to the general public in its present form. It is a pleasure to extend our thanks to Dr. Gordis' devoted friend, Dr. Abraham I. Shinedling, for his invaluable aid in seeing this volume through the press.

We pray that the insights reflected in the pages that follow will serve not only to increase our understanding but to hallow our lives as well.

MARVIN S. WIENER, *Director*
National Academy for Adult Jewish Studies
of the United Synagogue of America

Iyar 5727
May 1967

# An Age of Crisis

According to an ancient tradition, Adam once turned to Eve and said, "We are living in an age of revolution." That feeling has persisted among all their descendants. Every age has felt that the old verities were slipping and the world was changing. The older generation almost always believed that the changes were for the worse. The Romans had a phrase for it: *laudatores temporis acti,* "those who praise times gone by." The Biblical sage, Koheleth, warned against this weakness: "Do not say, 'What has happened, for the early days were better than these?' for not wisely have you asked the question" (Ecclesiastes 7:10).

Yet it is undeniable that ours is an age of multiple revolution, triple in character — scientific, socio-economic and moral. As a result of scientific and technological progress, our generation has reached a level of plenty and of peril previously undreamt of even in man's wildest fantasies. In turn, the greater material abundance of the mid-twentieth century has produced a revolution of rising expectations. Submerged groups and individuals are now unwilling to remain on a marginal or sub-marginal level of subsistence. This revolt takes on many aspects: racial conflict, the war against poverty at home, the Alliance for Progress in Latin America, and the revolt against colonialism in Africa and Asia. Finally, both these revolutions have united to produce a third: the current revolution in morals and standards of conduct.

In order to gauge the vast extent of this revolution in personal morality, we need to recall the traditional or official code of the Western world as preached by religion and enforced by law.

## The Traditional Code of Morality

Its basic principles may be set forth briefly:

A. *Parental hegemony in the patriarchal family.*

The father and mother have authority over their children during childhood and adolescence until they leave to be married and establish their own households. This condition prevailed during the greater portion of recorded history. During the rural stage in society when agriculture was the principal occupation, and in the earlier phases of the Industrial Revolution when the home served as a factory, the family was an economic unit. Here the role of the father as breadwinner and his effectiveness in his chosen field of endeavor were evident to the entire family, a situation which strengthened his authority and cemented family unity.

B. *The standard of chastity before marriage and fidelity during marriage.*

Intimate relations outside the marriage bond are forbidden. To be sure, the twentieth century has witnessed a steady increase in associations between young people and adults of both sexes in school, in business, in social life, and in the general community. There has accordingly developed a growing measure of freedom in personal relations everywhere, except for some ultra-traditional groups. In general, some measure of personal contact has been countenanced, even when not favored. Nevertheless, the standard continues to be upheld that intimate relations between the sexes are to be limited to marriage partners.

C. *Monogamy is the only acceptable marriage system.*

Some time ago, an Arab prince coming to the United States with several of his wives, was questioned about polygamy. He pointed out that the frequency of divorce in Western society has created what might be called "successive" as against "simultaneous" polygamy. The frequency of divorce notwithstanding, monogamy is the only recognized structure of marriage in the Western world.

These are the fundamentals of traditional morality, to which millions of men and women adhere faithfully. Were it otherwise, the entire fabric of our society would crumble. At the same time, it is undeniable that the code has been breached at many points. For untold numbers of our fellow men in our day, the realities of personal conduct and family morality are radically different from the official ideals of chastity and fidelity.

## A Revolution in Morals

Before we turn to the far-reaching changes that are taking place in contemporary life, a caveat is in order. It should not be inferred that the old order was ideal or that the new developments are totally retrograde. Any fair-minded student of human society will recognize that not infrequently the traditional moral code sanctioned — even when it did not create — situations marked by cruelty, oppression, suffering, and hypocrisy. The evidence is written large in literature and in the arts, as well as in history. In addition, it may be argued that some of the changes in personal and group morality that are now taking place are beneficial, or at least not harmful. What is important to recognize is that these transformations are propelled by powerful social and cultural forces, and that many of them are therefore inevitable and irreversible.

Basic to all aspects of the "new morality" is a *strong emphasis upon individual freedom and the fulfillment of personal desires.* As a result, the accepted moral code has been drastically modified or subverted.

## A. *Parental authority has all but disappeared.*

Today the rebellion of children begins in their teens, if not earlier, with regard to the hours they keep, their habits of study, their companions, and their personal behavior. Rarely are the parents willing or able to stem the tide of ever greater "permissiveness" characteristic of the modern temper.

A major factor in the breakdown of paternal authority is the fact that the family is no longer the scene of economic activity. The father's occupation is completely sundered from his wife and children, whose only interest in it lies in the money he derives from it and makes available to them. Hence the American father at home is often a ludicrous figure, as in the well-known comic strip, "Bringing Up Father." At best, he is tolerated rather than venerated. He has far less impact upon the molding of the character and behavior patterns of the children than has his wife.

Foreign observers have described "momism" as an American phenomenon, reaching its commercial climax on Mother's Day. "Momism" is a compensatory mechanism for the collapse of paternal authority in the modern home. But with more and more mothers fully employed, or involved in voluntary activities outside the home, even this source of parental influence is becoming eroded.

A new trend has been making considerable headway of late, particularly in the suburbs — but not only there. Young men and women, in college and out, are tending to leave the family home even before marriage and take an apartment for themselves. It is obvious that this step must lead to a drastic reduction of contacts with parents and, consequently, to a radical loss of parental influence.

After marriage it is taken for granted that the couple will be virtually free from parental "interference." I recall a couple who came in for a pre-marital conference. The young bride-to-be said in the most matter-of-fact tone, "Of course we want to live as far away as possible from Stan's parents and mine." This attitude is regarded as self-evident and perfectly natural. Hence parents or grandparents are likely to have little influence and certainly no authority in the lives of their children, after the children attain maturity.

B. *The concept of pre-marital continence is rapidly disappearing.*

When the Kinsey Report was published in 1958 indicating widespread divergence from the accepted code, an outcry of horror and disbelief greeted its appearance. Today its findings would no longer be regarded as sensational. We are assured by experts that intimate relations among young people, especially if they are in love and are engaged to be married to each other, are more likely to be the rule rather than the exception.

Many now live by what Ira Reiss, University of Iowa sociologist, calls "permissiveness with affection." What this means to most people is that: 1) morals are a private affair; 2) being in love justifies pre-marital sex and, by implication, perhaps extra-marital sex; and 3) nothing really is wrong as long as nobody else "gets hurt."[1]

The rapid rise in illegitimate births is a subject of mounting concern. This situation is by no means limited to minority groups in the United States. Dr. Ernest Claxton of the British Medical Association reports that one out of every six births in Britain today is illegitimate and that nearly two out of three babies born to women twenty years or younger are conceived outside of marriage. In the United States there were 265,000 illegitimate births in 1965—100,000 more than five years earlier. Approximately 50% of all teenage brides are pregnant before marriage and the percentage rises to 80% if both partners are teenagers. From 1940 to 1966, the official rate of illegitimate births trebled, from 7.1 to 23.4 births per 1,000 single women of childbearing age.[2] In Italy, where there is no civil divorce, it is estimated that there are five million Italians living in settled but irregular second unions. From 1952 to 1962, 28.6% of all live births in Italy were illegitimate, the vast majority to unmarried women.[3]

The abortion rate is rising at an alarming speed. For obvious reasons, no adequate statistics are available, but the number undoubtedly runs to hundreds of thousands annually, if not higher. In spite of the improved therapy available, venereal disease is on the increase. In England, the rise has equalled 45% in ten years. In the United States, the venereal disease rate among teenagers rose 5% in 1965 over the preceding year.[4]

Marital infidelity, which has, to be sure, always existed, is a widespread phenomenon of our times. Kinsey's research offered some statistical data on this phenomenon that were admittedly incomplete.

C. *Divorce has been constantly rising in America.*

In 1867 there were ten thousand divorces in the United States; in 1916 the number had grown elevenfold to one hundred and twelve thousand; in 1929 it had again almost doubled, to two hundred and one thousand. The economic depression which followed produced a temporary drop, due largely to the cost of securing a divorce in the face of the archaic laws prevailing in our country. The upward trend of divorces was resumed shortly thereafter. In 1937, there were two hundred fifty thousand divorces; in 1940, three hundred thousand; in 1948, four hundred fifteen thousand. More significantly, in the seventy-year period from 1870 to 1940 the American population increased threefold, marriages fourfold, and divorces twentyfold.

An acute social historian summarizes the changes of a half century with wit as well as with accuracy in these words: "Most of the elderly *grandes dames* at the resorts have lived from a day when they had to leave the room when the subject of divorce was mentioned, to a day when a wedding invitation has only approximately a fifty-fifty chance of being issued by parents of the same name as the bride."[5]

At present, divorces in the United States equal one-fourth of the number of marriages. The situation is even graver with youngsters. Fully 40% of American marriages involve teenagers and of these teenage marriages, 50% end in divorce in five years.[6]

To be sure, no ideal has ever been fully adhered to in practice. The traditional standards were always violated in the past. The great difference today is not merely quantitative — that the violations have increased in extent. It is qualitative — in the past, those who disobeyed the moral standards recognized that they were in the wrong; they did not attack the validity of the code they had broken. Until recently, when a man was on trial for a capital offense and the question of his sanity was involved, the McNaghten Rule would be invoked in order to determine whether the accused "could tell right from wrong." Today, in the area of personal morality, neither the defendant, nor the judge, nor the jury, nor the public can tell right from wrong! The code is not merely being disobeyed in practice, but disavowed in theory. What characterizes our age is not the violation of standards but the denial of these standards. In the words of Methodist Bishop Gerald Kennedy of Los Angeles, "The atmosphere is wide open. There is more promiscuity, and it is taken as a matter of course now by people. In my day they did it, but they knew it was wrong."[7]

## The Current Revolution — Its Causes

What are the causes for this far-reaching revolution? There is no reason for believing that men and women are more depraved than in the past. Human nature has not changed, but the conditions of human existence have been radically altered by the scientific and technological revolution and by the consequences that have come in its wake.

One obvious factor is the vastly enlarged mobility of modern man. In the Middle Ages the average peasant never travelled more than ten miles from his home during his entire lifetime. Even in modern times, most people have tended to live in one area all their lives. This is almost never the case today. People shift their economic class, their social contacts, their neighborhoods. As a result, they often lack a sense of roots. They tend to feel much less constrained by traditional patterns of behavior.

The impact of the automobile on morality can scarcely be exaggerated. It has worked a transformation in every aspect of contemporary life. It has created our suburbs, has spawned the motel, and offers far greater opportunities for freedom of conduct to men, women and young people.

An even more important factor in creating the new morality is the growth of women's independence. Over 50% of American women are now gainfully employed and the figure continues to rise. In addition, a high percentage of women are active in communal work and public service on a voluntary basis. Most American women are no longer secluded within their homes, which require less of their time and energy because of count-less labor-saving devices. As a result, women have far greater opportunities for contact and association with men outside the circle of their immediate family.

Even more basic is the fact that women are no longer dependent on marriage for their sustenance. The em-ployment market gives women the opportunity to "live alone and like it" or, at least to live alone, if the alter-natives seem less attractive. As a result, the "double standard" of morality is rapidly disappearing. Twenty-seven hundred years ago the prophet Hosea objected to the double standard: "I shall not punish your daughters when they play the harlot, or your daughters-in-law when they commit adultery. For the men themselves go aside with harlots and sacrifice with prostitutes, and a people without understanding shall come to ruin" (4:14). What is happening today is not that men have adopted the more rigorous standards traditional for women, but that women are tending to accept the freer norms of be-havior condoned for men.

Finally, several major deterrents to free sexual rela-tions have lost their power. The fear of venereal dis-ease has been reduced because more potent drugs are available. The technical devices for contraception have been vastly improved and are being far more widely disseminated. To be sure, these factors have not been totally eliminated, as is indicated by the growth of vene-real disease, the rise in illegitimate births, and the in-crease in the abortion rate. But it is possible today for young people, and older ones as well, to engage in freer sexual relations with considerably less fear of untoward physical and social consequences.

These new conditions have created a new outlook, often described as the "new morality." The truth is, however, that this is not a new outlook at all, but an inversion of the traditional view underlying Western civilization and derived from Christian theology. Basic to the Christian conception of sex, love and marriage, is an inner contradiction which is an important factor, though not the only one, in helping to create the ills in the present situation.

## *The Outlook of Classical Christianity*

The foundations of this outlook were laid by Paul in the New Testament. This approach became embodied in Christian doctrine and attained the status of law in Catholicism and, in somewhat lesser degree, in Protestantism as well. Increasingly, however, the practice of modern Christians has diverged from the ideals which they continue to profess. From this contradiction a spiritual schizophrenia has irrupted in the Western world.

Paul, the founder of Christianity, was born a Jew and regarded himself as "a Pharisee, son of a Pharisee" (Acts 23:6). But he was raised in the Greek city of Tarsus in Asia Minor and his outlook was molded by his Hellenistic environment. From the Greek culture surrounding him he derived his concept that there are two elements in a human being perpetually at war with one another — body and soul. The soul is immaterial, perfect and eternal. The body is gross, corruptible and the source of sin. It therefore follows that the highest type of human existence lies in transcending the physical and in living purely on the spiritual level. Hence the ideal state is

that of celibacy. Since, however, most people cannot
attain to this exalted level, marriage is created, basically
as a concession to the lower impulses of human nature.
Marriage is necessary for the procreation of the race and
can be justified in the eyes of God only on this basis and
for this purpose.

Paul's fullest discussion of the subject is to be found
in First Corinthians, chapter 7, the salient sections of
which read as follows:

"It is well for a man not to touch a woman. But because of the temptation to immorality, each man should
have his own wife and each woman her own husband.
The husband should give to his wife her conjugal rights,
and likewise the wife to her husband. . . .

"Do not refuse one another, except perhaps by agreement for a season, that you may devote yourselves to
prayer; but then come together again, lest Satan tempt
you through lack of self-control. I say this by way of
concession, not of command. I wish that all were as I
myself am. But each has his own special gift from God,
one of one kind and one of another.

"To the unmarried and the widows I say that it is
well for them to remain single as I do. But if they cannot exercise self-control, they should marry. For it is
better to marry than to be aflame with passion.

"To the married I give charge, not I but the Lord,
that the wife should not separate from her husband
(but if she does, let her remain single or else be recon-
ciled to her husband) and that the husband should not
divorce his wife. . . .

"I think that in view of the impending distress it is
well for a person to remain as he is. Are you bound to

a wife? Do not seek to be free. Are you free from a wife?
Do not seek marriage. But if you marry, you do not sin,
and if a girl marries she does not sin. Yet those who
marry will have worldly troubles, and I would spare you
that. . . .

"If any one thinks that he is not behaving properly
toward his betrothed, if his passions are strong, and it
has to be, let him do as he wishes; let them marry — it
is no sin. But whoever is firmly established in his heart,
being under no necessity but having his desire under
control, and has determined this in his heart, to keep
her as his betrothed, he will do well. So that he who
marries his betrothed does well; and he who refrains
from marriage will do better.

"A wife is bound to her husband as long as he lives.
If the husband dies, she is free to be married to whom
she wishes, only in the Lord. But in my judgment she
is happier if she remains as she is. And I think that I
have the Spirit of God."[8]

From this theory of sex as basically evil, and of marriage as a concession to the lower aspects of human
nature, flow several consequences:

Celibacy is regarded as the highest ideal, and is therefore obligatory for the priest, the monk and the nun.
As recently as 1952, Pope Pius XII "severely censured
those who, despite the Church's warnings and in con-
trast to her opinion, give marriage a preference in principle above virginity."[9]

Marriage is an estate which can be countenanced only
because it is essential to the perpetuation of the human
race, and hence it may be conceived of as a sacrament.
It is, however, also a concession to man's lower nature

and hence it must bear the stigma of a punishment.

This ambivalent attitude toward marriage has its parallel in the contradictory standpoint on divorce. From the logical point of view, if marriage is a concession to the physical impulses, release from this condition through divorce should have been facilitated, as marking a return to a higher "state of grace." That is emphatically not the case. For marriage is also a sacrament which cannot be dissolved except on the ground of adultery. Hence dissolution of the marriage bond is possible only through a criminal action, with divorce as the penalty meted out against the guilty party. If husband and wife are both agreed that living together is intolerable, they are guilty of collusion, a conspiracy against the law, and a divorce cannot be granted.

Since sexual relations are permissible only when they can lead to the begetting of children, the practice of birth control through chemical or mechanical means is regarded as sinful and forbidden. Only abstinence, or reliance upon "the rhythm method," when conception is less likely to take place, is permissible. To justify this standpoint, a Biblical passage, Genesis 38:9 f., is invoked — and misinterpreted — to justify the theological odium placed upon sexual relations without the possibility of procreation. Actually the Biblical context makes it clear that Onan's sin was his unwillingness to fulfill his fraternal duty of raising up offspring to bear his dead brother's name.

It is obvious that attitudes such as these, aside from their inherent contradictions, were bound to come into conflict with the many problems, opportunities and temptations confronting men and women, particularly in modern society. As a result, Protestantism, which never officially surrendered the New Testament attitudes, accepted their attenuation in practice. Celibacy was abandoned as the ideal state, and divorce was tacitly recognized as permissible on various grounds. The pressures for family limitations became increasingly imperious, and Protestantism did not oppose the planned parenthood movement. Indeed, church leaders found it not only legitimate but morally incumbent under various circumstances.

The Roman Catholic Church, on the other hand, has continued to reaffirm vigorously the New Testament standpoint to the present day. Yet the inexorable march of events has weakened this point of view even among Catholics. All birth control clinics report large numbers of otherwise devoted Catholics who utilize their services. A nationwide study in 1965 based on interviews with 5,600 married women of all faiths indicated that a majority of Roman Catholic wives between the ages of 18 and 39 no longer conform to church doctrine on birth control. It was reported that the proportion of Catholic wives complying with the church's ban on contraceptives had declined from 70% in 1955 to 62% in 1960 and 47% in 1965. Moreover, defiance of church doctrine by Catholic wives included a large proportion of women who report regular church attendance. For those who go to mass every week, conformity with doctrine has plummeted from 78% in 1955 to 69% in 1960 and to 56% in 1965, a pattern matching the rate of decline for Catholic women as a whole.[10]

At the Second Vatican Council, a commission was appointed by Pope John XXIII to restudy the traditional Catholic teaching on the subject. Pope Paul VI enlarged the commission, which was authoritatively reported to have favored authorizing the use of anovulants — the so-called birth control pill. Many members of the commission were prepared to go further and to permit the use of mechanical contraceptives as well. Nevertheless, Pope Paul, on October 28, 1966, restated the traditional prohibition for Catholics and declared that he "must defer any modification still for some time."[11]

These specific implications flowing out of the traditional Christian outlook in such areas as celibacy, divorce and birth control are obviously highly important for Christian believers, even in this era of flux. Yet the New Testament teaching is even more significant for modern society as a whole, because it has molded the basic approach toward morality that is characteristic of Western man, whether he be Christian or "post-Christian" in his conscious world-view.

The traditional outlook on sex as evil has created the concept that love becomes higher, the less it is involved in sex. Love is holy, but sex is low; love is pure, but sex is unclean. In the Middle Ages, the ideal of knightly love was a love never physically consummated, as in the romance of Tristan and Isolde. Romeo and Juliet are star-crossed lovers whose passion for each other is never gratified. In the world of reality, Dante and Beatrice, who saw each other only a few times during their lifetime and never established any personal relationship, symbolized the highest type of love attachment.

In the modern period, "romantic love" has been glorified in song, literature, on the screen and on the stage, and has become a dominant element of our culture. In

essence, it is a secularized version of the Christian love
ideal, for romantic love *par excellence* is unfulfilled or
incomplete love, the passion experienced either before
marriage or outside of it.[12] Modern society, particularly
in America, regards "love" as the essential, indeed often
as the all-sufficient basis for entering into marriage, and
the results are written large in the mounting divorce
statistics.

## The "New Morality" and Its Consequences

It becomes clear that the "old sanctities" of the traditional code and the "new morality" of modern behavior
agree on one fundamental. While it is impossible, for
obvious reasons, to sever love and sex completely in
practice, the effort is made to keep them as far apart as
possible, at least in theory. Actually, the modern view
is an inversion of the traditional standpoint. Traditional
morality glorifies love and declares that sex is, or should
be, irrelevant and unrelated to love. The modern age
glorifies sex and maintains that love is, or should be,
irrelevant and unrelated to sex. Many modern men and
women have therefore drawn the conclusion that sexual
experience is permissible even where there is no love.

In sum, a far freer code of sexual morality has emerged,
for two reasons. First, new conditions have made it prac-
ticable, and second, a theory is available to justify it,
derived from the inherent contradictions of classic
Christian teaching.

What is highly significant in our age of disbelief is
that this view of sex as inherently evil has persisted even
after Christian doctrine has lost its hold upon many of

its devotees. The conviction that sex is immoral, if not sinful, continues to survive in the world-view — and, what is even more important, in the emotional make-up — of non-believers. Frequently heretics who have surrendered the basic dogmas of traditional Christianity on the conscious level continue to retain subconsciously the negative attitude toward sex inherited from Paul and his patristic successors.[13] As a result, many modern men and women who have lost the sense of sin continue to be oppressed by feelings of guilt. It is one of the great insights of modern psychoanalysis that psychological disturbances of varying intensity, running the full gamut from minor neurosis to major psychosis, are induced by contradictions in the human psyche between conscious attitudes and subconscious feelings.

It is no accident that our society exhibits a deep-seated schizophrenia — sentimental glorification of "love" on the one hand and widespread pornography, prostitution and promiscuity on the other. All these unhealthy manifestations have arisen because the sex code preached by traditional religion and embodied in contemporary law all too often runs counter to the promptings of human nature. What has been driven out through the door comes in through the window, with one tragic difference: the visitor is no longer a respectable caller, amenable to law and order, but a surreptitious law-breaker. Untold numbers of men and women who no longer accept the outlook of the traditional religion in which they were reared and often have broken violently with the morality based upon it, remain subject to its compulsions, and never more strongly than when they flout its teachings in word or in deed.

Obviously, the present situation is poles apart from the traditional concepts of personal and family morality. But if it were true that the "new morality" adds to the sum total of human happiness and well-being, we might argue that the time has come to surrender the accepted code in favor of a new approach. All the evidence, however, points in the opposite direction — men and women are not happier under the new dispensation.

The appalling rate of divorce continues to grow. While Judaism does not consider divorce a sin, it recognizes it as a tragedy. Each divorce is a tombstone on high hopes once held by two young people — hopes for happiness, contentment and love that have dissolved in bitterness and hostility. The unhappiness of the adult partners is only one part of this massive burden of misery. There are hundreds of thousands of innocent victims of discord, the children of divorce, who lack the security and the guidance of two parents and a stable home.

Even more tragic is the mass of suffering involved in the rising tide of illegitimate births. No one can contemplate without trembling the fear and shame of a mother who bears an unwanted child, and the even heavier sense of deprivation of the child who has never known a father and who, throughout his life, carries a stigma for which he is not responsible.

Worst of all is the phenomenon of abortion, which is generally illegal, except in carefully circumscribed circumstances. Here is a staggering mass of human suffering, of danger and death for mothers and for offspring yet unborn.

There are millions of men and women, to be sure, whose lives are free from the experience of divorce, illegitimate births or abortions, but even their happiness in marriage cannot be taken for granted. That so large a percentage of our population lacks and hungers desperately for a measure of serenity in life is clear from the increasing use of LSD and other hallucinatory drugs, marijuana, pep pills, and sedatives by millions of men, women and young people.

In sum, it is not merely that the present practice runs counter to traditional morality; it has not made people better or happier. Unless all signs fail, *lo zeh ha-derekh*, "that is not the way."

## The Jewish Concept of Sex

Is there any guidance to be found in Jewish tradition that can help extricate men and women from the mass of misery in the most intimate and basic area of experience? Before we explore the resources of Judaism we must restate several fundamental principles. Though the concept of a Judeo-Christian heritage has been challenged in some quarters, it possesses genuine value. Elsewhere I have sought to delineate the contents and limits of the traditions of Judaism and Christianity.[14] However, recognizing the validity of the concept is not to imply that Jewish teaching is identical with that of Christianity. Especially in the field of family morality as well as in several other areas, the Jewish tradition has something distinctive and valuable to contribute to the modern world.[15]

Moreover, Jewish tradition is not a rivulet, but a mighty stream with many currents, large and small. It possesses a mainstream as well as lesser influences that must be evaluated properly and correctly, if we are to find it a fountain of "living waters" rather than a mass of congealed ice.

It must also be recognized that not all stages of the Jewish historic experience are of equal significance. The great creative periods were the eras of the Bible and the Talmud, when Jews were in contact with the great Oriental and Greco-Roman civilizations. In the Middle Ages, when Jews lived under vastly more constricted conditions, their outlook was influenced by the far narrower world-view of medieval Christianity and by the tragic limitations and perils of their own ghetto existence. Hence, in the Middle Ages there emerged a Jewish attitude toward sex and the family which was a mixture of the life-affirming Biblical-Talmudic attitude on the one hand, and the medieval emphasis upon asceticism and the negation of the natural on the other.

In ascertaining the teaching of the Jewish tradition, it is therefore important to ask not merely where does Jewish tradition *stand*, but whither does it *move*? What is the spirit, the goal of Jewish tradition? If we are not content to know Judaism superficially but seek to understand it from within, it is important to recognize not merely its position but its direction, its thrust and goal.

When these canons are kept in mind, it becomes clear that Judaism has vital insights and attitudes to offer modern men and women in the area of personal conduct and family morality.

Judaism has a healthy-minded, affirmative attitude toward sex, which it recognizes as an essential and legitimate element of human life. Since God created man with his entire complement of impulses, sex is a manifestation of the Divine. It is therefore neither to be glorified, as in the exaggerations of romantic love, nor denigrated, as in classic Christian theology.

The Bible and the Talmud are frank and outspoken in dealing with the sexual component of human experience. The pages of our classic literature are free both from obscenity and false modesty, from pornography and comstockery, which are essentially two sides of the same coin.

In the medieval mystical treatise *Iggeret Ha-kodesh*, attributed to Nahmanides, the classic Jewish attitude is clearly and vigorously expressed: "We who are the descendants of those who received the sacred Torah believe that God, blessed be He, created everything as His wisdom dictated, and He created nothing containing obscenity or ugliness *(genai o kiyyur)*. For if we were to say that intercourse *(ha-hibbur)* is obscene, it would follow that the sexual organs are obscene. . . . And how could God, blessed be He, create something containing a blemish or obscenity, or a defect; for we would then find that His deeds are not perfect, though Moses, the greatest of the prophets, proclaims and says, 'The Rock, whose work is perfect' (Deuteronomy 32:4). However, the fact is, as it is said, that 'God is pure-eyed, so that He sees no evil' (Habakkuk 1:13). Before Him there is neither degradation nor obscenity; He created man and woman, fashioning all their organs and setting them in their proper function, with nothing obscene in them."[16]

Since sex and love are indissolubly linked, the term *ahavah* is used both for the physical and the spiritual aspects of love. The Christian theologians are wont to emphasize the fact — and take pride in it — that there are two Greek terms for "love": *eros*, representing "carnal love," and *agape*, meaning "charity, spiritual love." The Hebrew outlook, on the contrary, finds it entirely proper to apply the same root, *ahav*, to all aspects of love. The ideal relationship of man to God ("You shall love the Lord your God"), the love of one's fellow man ("You shall love your neighbor as yourself") and the love of man and woman ("How fair and how pleasant you are, O love, with its delights!") are all expressed by the same Hebrew root.[17]

The Song of Songs in the Bible is a superb, lyrical anthology containing songs of love and nature, of courtship and marriage, which glorify the physical aspects of love and reveal its spiritual character. That the Song of Songs was admitted to the Biblical canon is evidence of the persistence in Judaism of the basic conception that the natural is holy. In John Donne's words, "Love's mysteries in souls do grow, but yet the body is his book." If the two basic imperatives of religion are the love of God and the love of man, the Song of Songs, no less than the book of Psalms, deserves its place in Scripture.[18]

It is true that the Rabbis of the Talmud explained the Song of Songs as an allegory, and that this interpretation was undoubtedly decisive in having it enter the Biblical canon. Nonetheless the Sages were well aware of its literal meaning. Thus Rabbi Akiba, who described the Song of Songs as "the Holy of Holies," issued the warning, "He who gives his voice a flourish in reading the Song of

Songs in the banquet halls and makes it a secular song
has no share in the world to come." [19] For the same reason, some of the Sages expressed doubts regarding the
canonicity of the Song. [20] That the Song deals with the
love of man and woman is implicitly recognized in the
statement of Rabbi Jonathan, "Solomon wrote the Song
of Songs in his youth, then Proverbs, then Ecclesiastes.
This is the way of the world. When a man is young,
he writes songs; when he gets older, he writes proverbs;
when he is old, he says, 'all is vanity.' "[21]

The Talmud devotes one of the most extensive of its
six sections (*Nashim*, "Women"), as well as many passages in other sections, to marriage law and personal
morality, and the post-Talmudic Codes maintain the
tradition. This detailed preoccupation in the Halakhah
with all aspects of sexual life, even the most intimate,
testifies to the recognition that "this too is Torah and
one must learn." [22]

Judaism has a realistic understanding of the power of
sex, both for good and evil. Rabbinic sources generally
refer to it as *yetzer ha-ra*, "the evil impulse," because
they recognize how often the sexual impulse becomes a
source of evil, leading men to violate the dictates of reason and the canons of morality, overriding their ideals
and distorting the pattern of their lives.

Yet the mere translation of the term *yetzer ha-ra* as
"the evil impulse" does not do justice to the breadth of
understanding in Jewish tradition. Long before modern
psychoanalysis, Rabbinic Judaism was aware of the central role of sex in civilization: "Were it not for the sexual
impulse (literally, the evil impulse), no man would build
a house or marry a woman or engage in an occupation." [23]

The role of sex in stimulating men to activity and thus furthering human progress is mirrored in another Rabbinic epithet, "the leaven in the dough." Like the more common term, "evil impulse," this term is at times used simply as a designation for the sexual proclivities of men.[24] Leaven is ferment — it may bring decay, but it is also the source of growth.

In a charming and witty tale, the Talmud ridicules the fear of the evil impulse, which characterized some ascetic groups during the period of the Second Temple. The Rabbis tell that the Men of the Great Synagogue were greatly exercised by the evil brought into the world by the *yetzer ha-ra*. In response to their importunities, "the evil impulse" was handed over to them and they proceeded to imprison him for thirty days. As a result, not an egg could be found in all the land. They could not kill him, lest they be destroyed, nor would Heaven agree to cut his power in half. Finally, they blinded one of his eyes and released him, thus reducing but not eliminating his hold upon men.[25]

The Rabbis did not hesitate to interpret the great Commandment, "You shall love the Lord your God with all your heart" to mean "with your two impulses — the good impulse and the evil impulse."[26] Thus, sex becomes an instrument for the fulfillment of the love of God, a powerful force that can be channelled for good, in spite of its capacity for evil.

The attitude of traditional Judaism in its great creative periods may therefore be summarized as a denial that man's nature *eo ipso* is evil, whether as a result of Adam's sin, or because of any theoretical distinction between body and soul, or on any other ground.[27] The judgment on Creation in Genesis 1:31: "And God saw all that He had made, and behold it was very good," was unflinchingly taken by the Rabbis to include even death itself.[28]

It therefore follows that man's nature, all of which is the handiwork of God, is good, actually or potentially. Man's misuse of any of his instincts or faculties constitutes his own sin, *het*, "missing the mark" for which he should have aimed and which he could have reached.

Judaism has always remained realistically aware of man's proclivity to evil, of which the sexual impulse is perhaps the most powerful manifestation, though by no means the only one. "Two impulses God created in His world, the impulse to idolatry (*avodah zarah*) and the impulse to immorality (*zenut*). The impulse to idolatry has already been uprooted, but the impulse to immorality still remains. God said, 'Whoever can resist the second is considered as though he resisted both.' " [29] Nevertheless, Jewish tradition insists that, like all other attributes of human nature, the sexual impulse *per se* is neutral. It can be utilized as an instrument for building or for destroying the world. Thus Judaism avoids the Scylla of unbridled license characteristic of modern paganism and the Charybdis of the condemnation of sex to be found in traditional Christianity.

## Marriage in the Jewish Tradition

Judaism regards marriage and not celibacy as the ideal human state, because it alone offers the opportunity for giving expression to all aspects of human nature. Speaking of his celibacy, Paul said, "I would that all men were as I." But when the sage Simeon ben Azzai did not marry, he felt constrained to apologize by saying, "My soul loves the Torah," explaining that he wished to dedicate himself wholeheartedly to study without worldly concerns.[30] His practice was emphatically the exception, not the rule, in Jewish life.

The Hebrew legal term for marriage, *kiddushin*, was popularly interpreted, quite in the spirit of the tradition, as "the state of holiness." From its inception, Judaism has always recognized two purposes in marriage, both spelled out in the opening pages of Scripture.

The first is the fulfillment of the first commandment: "Be fruitful and multiply" (Genesis 1:28). Children are uniformly regarded as a blessing. The Bible is replete with references to children as God's greatest boon. From Abraham's passionate cry, "What can You give me, if I die childless?", to the 128th Psalm, with its idyllic picture of the family gathered around the table, there is a consistent emphasis upon children as a good. Undoubtedly, economic considerations played their part, for children were additional workers and defenders of the family fortunes. Yet more fundamental is the instinctive desire for children, as constituting man's renewal and immortality. The Talmud expresses this feeling when it says: "Four are considered dead: the poor, the blind, the leper, and he who has no children."[31]

The commandment "Be fruitful and multiply" is defined by the Halakhah with characteristic minuteness. The obligation is fulfilled as soon as two children are born, the only question being whether two boys are necessary, as the school of Shammai insists, or one boy and one girl, as Hillel avers.[32]

The procreation of children is a basic goal of marriage, but it is not the only one. It is noteworthy that in the Bible, Eve is created for Adam before procreation is contemplated, while they are still in the Garden of Eden. The second function of marriage is that of companionship. Actually, it is the only motive assigned in the creation of a helpmate for Adam: "It is not good for man to dwell alone; I will make a helpmate for him" (Genesis 2:18).

That companionship, which includes sexual relations, is a legitimate end in itself in marriage, is not merely an implication of the Biblical story but is explicitly spelled out in Jewish law. The Halakhah teaches that weak, old and sterile persons should marry, even when there is no possibility of children.[33] Thus the Rabbis could endorse wholeheartedly the sentiment of a modern sociologist: "Sex exists not only for the propagation of the race, but for the increase of individual human happiness."[34]

While a negative attitude toward sexual relations is sporadically encountered in Jewish literature, particularly under the impact of medieval asceticism and pietism, it is far from representing the normative view. Basically, sexual relations between husband and wife, while naturally private and intimate, are held to be a perfectly legitimate form of pleasure which justifies itself as such, even without the goal of procreation.

Indeed, Judaism holds fast to two complementary concepts in this area. First is the ideal of *tzeniyut*, which can be translated only imperfectly as "modesty, propriety, delicacy, good taste." This ideal is expected to govern men and women in their dress, their speech and their conduct to all, publicly and within the privacy of their homes.[35] At the same time, Judaism regards it not merely as permissible but as mandatory for a man and his wife to derive pleasure from the sexual act, which has been ordained by God, and by that token is holy. Thus Jewish tradition established the practice of the husband's reading the Song of Songs on the Sabbath eve,[36] and the Halakhah spells out the woman's conjugal rights in marriage, which are explicitly indicated in the Biblical text.[37] The Talmudic injunction that scholars and their wives have conjugal relations on Sabbath eve is explained by Rashi on the ground that the Sabbath is "for pleasure, rest and physical enjoyment." Nahmanides justifies the rule on mystical grounds, since a holy act should be performed on a holy day.[38]

While Catholicism considers various irregular forms of sexual play between man and wife as sinful and includes them in the confessional, Judaism holds that they are all permissible, although it favors the more normal form, lest these others become habitual and exclusive.[39]

Ideally, every human being should live as a unit within a family, for the family is the ideal human group. The Rabbis declare that he who has no wife is deprived of joy, of blessing, of all good, and lacks Torah and protection and peace.[40] A particularly moving comment expresses this ideal of companionship and equality: "He who loves his wife as himself and honors her more than

himself, of him Scripture declares, 'You shall know that
your tent is at peace' (Job 5:24)."[41]

Today, Catholic circles are hailing the discovery that
the purposes of marriage include companionship as well
as procreation. We can sympathize with our Catholic
friends as they wrestle to overcome the burden of Paul's
teaching in this area. But this insight is no recent inno-
vation in Judaism.

## Judaism and Birth Control

In contradistinction to official Catholic teaching —
which has now been reaffirmed, at least for the present —
Judaism does not stigmatize birth control as inherently
sinful. To be sure, Judaism has little sympathy for hus-
bands and wives who seek to avoid the responsibilities
involved in the rearing of children for the sake of ad-
vancing their own pleasure and ease. Yet it recognizes
that there are conditions under which avoiding the begetting of children is socially desirable.

A classical passage in the Talmud, repeated no less
than six times in Rabbinic literature,[42] discusses the
practice of family limitation: "Three types of women
practice contraception[43]: a child wife, lest she become
pregnant and die; a pregnant woman, lest her embryo
be injured and become an abortion; and a nursing
mother, lest she wean her child too soon and it die."[44]

The post-Talmudic commentators differ as to whether
these three types of women *may* practice family limitation
(and others may not), or whether these categories *must*
do so (and others may).[45] On either view, the existence
of a strong sanction is clear.

Talmudic law permits a woman to sterilize herself permanently, like the wife of the sage, Rabbi Hiyya, who "drank a cup" to render herself incapable of child-bearing, because she could not bear the extreme pain involved.[46] Rabbinic law also permitted women to avoid pregnancy if they had immoral or degenerate children, and feared bringing others of a similar kind into the world.[47]

From these passages it is clear that there is considerable warrant in Judaism for regarding limitation in the procreation of children as permissible, or even as obligatory, in cases where the mother's health is in danger or she is exposed to extraordinary pain, or the health of a child — born or unborn — would be jeopardized by this pregnancy. Finally, the tradition reckons with the danger of a poor heredity or environment.

In sum, Judaism regards the procreation of children as a God-given duty. It may, however, be set aside when it conflicts with the supreme Divine imperative, "He shall live by them — and not perish by them," which commands us to preserve existing human life and enhance it.[48]

To be sure, the more liberal attitude of Talmudic Judaism became constricted in the medieval period, which continued for East-European Jewry virtually until the twentieth century. Several factors conspired to transform the attitude toward family limitation by Jewish leadership during the Middle Ages and beyond. Throughout these centuries, persecution, spoliation, expulsion, and massacre made great inroads in the Jewish population. The physical hazards of disease and malnutrition also decimated the ranks of children.

Faced by these perils, medieval Jewry saw its preservation dependent on a high birth rate, without restriction or qualification. The imperious demand for group survival showed no consideration for individual desires or family welfare. Only through children and more children could the Jew hope to overcome the tragic mortality rate. Thus the instinctive wish for progeny was intensified by overpowering religio-national motives.

Hence the view of the Halakhah that the birth of two children fulfills the requirements of the Law was ignored. Parents were encouraged to bring as many children into the world as possible, with the hope that many, if not most of them, might survive the rigors of malnutrition, disease and persecution, and attain to maturity. The Talmudic passage permitting family limitation, which has been quoted above, was also interpreted in as strict a manner as possible.[49] Its clearcut provisions for the protection of the life and health of the mother and child were disregarded and often passed over in silence by later authorities.[50] A deep-seated opposition to birth control became dominant among traditionally-minded Jews, in spite of Jewish tradition. Nevertheless, in the Rabbinic Responsa of the eighteenth and nineteenth centuries, more liberal viewpoints are met with, side by side with more rigorous ones. But the spirit of the Jewish tradition, as experienced in its classic sources, remains clear.

Family limitation has one other great virtue, of which Judaism is particularly conscious. It permits earlier marriages. Our economic system often demands that both husband and wife work, at least for the first few years of their marriage. The Rabbis of the Talmud were refreshingly free from the modern hypocrisy which shuts its eyes to the danger of late marriages and pretends that most men and women can and will remain continent until middle age without negative consequences. Though traditional Judaism would have no sympathy for men and women who are physically and economically capable of rearing a family and refuse to do so because of selfishness or indolence, it would also not ignore the contention that it is better for reluctant parents not to bring unwanted children into the world.

Today, modern Judaism unequivocally reaffirms the obligation to perpetuate the human race through the medium of the family as a basic and general goal. But it recognizes also that family planning is a necessity of modern life, in view of complex moral, hygienic and economic factors.

As we have seen, Jewish law approaches the issue of birth control like the average family, from the standpoint of the individuals involved. In our day, however, another factor of overriding importance has entered into the situation — the world-wide "population explosion."[51] United Nations experts estimate that in the year 2000 there will be six billion people on the earth. This is double the present total, which itself is three times the size of the world population at the beginning of the century! The U.S. Bureau of the Census projects a population of 378,219,000 for the United States in the year 2000.[52]

The population explosion threatens the underdeveloped countries with total disaster. Their present food supply, already stretched thin, will be even less able to keep pace with the growing population tide, even if food resources are increased. The spectre of widespread hunger and disease affecting hundreds of millions on this planet is therefore a virtual certainty, if present trends continue.

Even the prosperous industrialized nations, who may be able to cope with the food problem, though this is doubtful, are confronted by major difficulties. The land available will not grow in extent. As a result, the problems of overcrowding and noise, of water and air pollution, which already constitute a massive complex of problems for our urbanized civilization, will become insoluble.

Faced by this menace, governmental programs of birth control have been launched in India and China, as well as in Pakistan, South Korea, Taiwan, Malaysia (in Asia) and in Egypt, Tunisia and Kenya (in Africa). Latin America, which has the largest rate of population growth in the world (2.8% a year against a world average of 2%), has lagged in birth control efforts. According to the Population Council, Latin America has resisted birth control "in part because of the predominantly Catholic religion and in part because of the countries' traditional image of themselves as under-populated, with large areas capable of new settlement." [53] There are signs, however, that this situation may be changing. Government-supported family planning campaigns have been launched in Chile, Honduras, Venezuela, Peru, and Jamaica. In Colombia, a nongovernmental birth control drive has started.

It is clear that birth control is essential if the population explosion is not to destroy man nearly as effectively as the atomic bomb. It is significant that Jewish tradition, with its blending of realism and idealism, once again demonstrates that it is a *torat hayyim,* "a law of life" for mankind.

## Non-Marital Relations

Judaism maintains the principle that sexual relations are proper only within the marriage bond.[54] As is well known, the Seventh Commandment categorically forbids adultery, the offspring of which bear the stigma of illegitimacy *(mamzerut)* in Jewish law.[55] Judaism also objects to all extra-marital relations. However, when they do not involve a married woman, it does not equate them with adultery or treat them as equally serious infractions of morality. Thus Jewish law does not regard a child born out of wedlock as illegitimate, though he obviously possesses an inferior social status *(shetuki).*[56]

Judaism is also opposed to pre-marital relations. While it shows a realistic insight into the human impulses involved,[57] it does not condone or sanction such relationships.[58]

It need hardly be pointed out that in traditional Jewish life, aberrations such as these from the ideals of chastity and fidelity were few and far between. Jewish leadership, therefore, rarely felt called upon to admonish or castigate the people with regard to the maintenance of personal morality. For centuries the lofty standards of Jewish family life have evoked the admiration of the world.

Nonetheless, the high level of insight into human nature and the sympathy for human weakness characteristic of the Jewish tradition are of special interest in our day when the situation is in radical flux.

In this connection, it is noteworthy that on October 15, 1966, a report was submitted by a commission established by the British Council of Churches dealing with these frontier issues in contemporary morality. The seventy-seven-page document entitled "Sex and Morality" created a furor, because "it declined to state unequivocally that sexual relations outside marriage are invariably wrong." [59] After considerable debate, the report was accepted, with the significant reaffirmation that sexual relations are permissible only in marriage. Yet the change of spirit and approach is unmistakable.

## The Jewish Attitude Toward Divorce

When a marriage has failed and all efforts to achieve compatibility and work a reconciliation prove useless, Judaism regards divorce as legitimate, even without a crime having been committed by one of the partners. This attitude is by no means identical with the accepted mores of our times. The contemporary American attitude toward divorce may be summarized as *official severity in law and total laxity in life*. It is the consequence of the tragic paradox in attitude which regards marriage as a necessary evil and divorce as a punishment for trying to escape the evil!

Traditional Judaism accepts the diametrically opposite attitude toward divorce. Instead of *severity in law and laxity in life*, Judaism establishes the contrary balance: *the attitude in life toward divorce is strict*, thus underscoring the need for the couple to strive earnestly for the permanence of the marriage bond, but *the law on divorce is liberal,* offering release where life together proves intolerable. All the resources of the tradition, the sanctity of its ideals and the solemnity of its ritual are invoked to make husband and wife recognize the sacred character of their union. "He who divorces his first wife — even the Temple altar sheds tears for him," the Rabbis declared.[60] The *Ketubah,* or marriage agreement, which requires a cash payment on the dissolution of a marriage, was instituted to hinder easy divorces. The same motive led to a complicated ritual with regard to the issuance of a bill of divorce *(get).*[61]

But once it becomes clear that the marriage has failed irremediably, Judaism recognizes that the union has lost its sanction and its sanctity, for love and mutual respect are the only marks of God's presence in a home. When these conditions do not obtain, the husband and wife are no longer joined together by God in any meaningful sense, and society stultifies itself by trying to ignore the truth.[62]

Nor does the presence of children necessarily mean that the marriage must be preserved at all costs. There is mounting evidence today that the happiness of the children, too, is often better served by a divorce than by a hate-ridden, quarrel-filled marriage.[63] Here again, Jewish tradition has manifested a deep insight into the realities of human nature, a level of understanding with which our age has scarcely begun to catch up.

In sum, Jewish law regards divorce not as a punishment for a crime but simply as a frank recognition that the marriage is unsuccessful. The grounds upon which a divorce is issued are therefore not limited to adultery. The fact that both parties recognize that they cannot live together happily, or at least tolerably well, constitutes the strongest ground for issuing a divorce, not for denying it. Rabbinic law lists many possible causes for divorce, including incompatibility of temperament, personal habits, or occupation. Any one of these may be invoked by the husband in issuing a divorce, or by the wife in suing for divorce before the Rabbinic courts.

Many of these grounds might seem superficial and unimportant to an outsider. Such is the charge that the wife burns the meals she serves, or that the husband suffers from bad breath or from an unpleasant disease, or that his occupation is distasteful to her.

Particularly striking is Rabbi Akiba's utterance that a man may divorce his wife "if he finds another more attractive." [64] Rabbi Akiba, it need hardly be added, was not defending promiscuity or the multiple-marriage pattern of some of the upper layers of modern society. His own marriage is one of the great love idylls of the Jewish tradition. But in admitting these grounds for divorce, Rabbi Akiba, like Judaism generally, shows a fine psychological perception of the reality of human relations. That such apparently superficial motives would be adduced by either party in order to secure a divorce is evidence of a deeper clash of personality between husband and wife, testimony that the community of spirit, which is the essence of marriage, has ceased to exist.

The effect of the Jewish law of divorce must be seen within the context of traditional Jewish life. In the Jewish community, powerful religious and social factors operated to heighten the sense of the sanctity of marriage and the conviction that a marriage was normally a permanent status. As a result, divorce was rarely resorted to, and only after all efforts at mutual adjustment and reconciliation had proved abortive. Thus, a fine balance existed between life, on the one hand, which stressed the sanctity and permanence of marriage, and the law, on the other, which had a remedy available in case of dire necessity, if all else proves fruitless.

*The moral imperative of Judaism is to strive to re-establish the sense of the sanctity of marriage as the noblest estate in which a man and woman can find themselves. Man fulfills himself most truly in marriage because marriage permits love to be united with responsibility, stamps it with the attribute of permanence and exemplifies the truth that sex and love are indivisible. It is preeminently in marriage that sex becomes holy and love becomes real.*

To be sure, Judaism has not solved all the problems in this area of personal conduct and family morality. No system of law or ethics can work perfectly, in view of the boundless variations and limitless weaknesses of human nature. In the words of Jeremiah, "The heart is deceitful above all else and very weak — who can know it?" (17:9). Yet Jewish teaching in this area is sane, balanced and workable, because it blends realistic understanding with idealistic aspiration.

## Unfinished Business — Women's Rights

Traditional Judaism, in particular, has an agenda of unfinished business in this area. While the entire trend of Jewish tradition moves in the direction of the extension of the rights of women, the process is not complete either in religion or in life. The full enfranchisement of women and their recognition as equals will not take place unless the women themselves demand, press and fight for equality. This is the very essence of the outlook of Conservative Judaism.

Jewish marriage and divorce procedures have not yet come to grips with the tragic reality of the *agunah*, "the abandoned wife," which has always aroused the compassion of Jewish religious leaders, but is far more acute today.[65] Conservative Judaism believes in the innate power for growth and development to be found in Jewish law. We have the august authority of the late Professor Louis Ginzberg, who declared that a remedy for the tragedy of the *agunah* can be found in Jewish law.

The new *Ketubah*, approved by Professor Saul Lieberman and utilized by many members of the Rabbinical Assembly, represents an important first step designed to minimize the suffering visited upon observant Jewish women by the difficulty they often encounter in securing a Jewish religious divorce. It should be understood that the injustice to which they are exposed in this area is due not to the inherent inequities of Jewish law, but to the inability of the Rabbinical court to enforce its provisions in a secular society. This was emphatically not the case in the autonomous Jewish community in the past, when the Jewish courts could compel obedience.

In view of changed circumstances, more vigorous steps can and should be taken to rectify the abuses that have grown up. It is intolerable that untold Jewish women in this position are confronted by the temptation to violate Jewish law, if they reach out for personal happiness. The law of God must be a law of justice and equality for all. The resources available within Jewish law have not failed — they have not yet been tried.

## The Sanctity of Marriage

We need to devote greater attention to the teaching of the Jewish concept of marriage and morality. In the face of the countless temptations which modern life affords, the subject can no longer be ignored. Jewish ethical insights and attitudes on sex and the family must be introduced into our schools, our camps, the program of our young people's organizations, our sisterhoods and men's clubs. Above all, the systematic study of Jewish values in this area should enter the field of youth and adult education. Time was when the whole area of sex education could be left in the hands of parents with a fair hope of success. Today, parents themselves are left with only the tattered remnants of a code. They cannot be expected to transmit to their children the authentic content of the tradition with the requisite knowledge, insight and sympathy.

Ernest Hemingway once issued a one-sentence manifesto: "What is moral is what you feel good after; what is immoral is what you feel bad after." This is indeed a satisfactory explanation, if we understand the word "after" to mean not "ten minutes or a half-hour after," but "long after" — that is to say, from the long-range point of view, when all the consequences of the act become clear.

Very similarly, Henry L. Mencken once sarcastically defined "conscience" as "a still, small voice that tells us that someone is looking." This, too, is a perfect definition, if we write the word "Someone" with a capital S! To inculcate the sense of the sanctity of marriage must become a basic enterprise for the teachers and exemplars of a living religion.

In addition to an educational program on sex and family morality, our congregations and sisterhoods ought to establish, on all age levels, a broadly-based system of personal counselling, before, during and after marriage. In these centers the technical knowledge and scientific skill of the psychologist would be enriched by the ideals of the Jewish tradition expounded by the scholars and rabbis, who would apply them with insight and sympathy to the problems of fallible human beings. Such Counselling Institutes might well be sponsored by several congregations in a given locality acting jointly to underwrite the program.

Only if we recapture the religious attitude toward marriage as a compact in which not two, but three, partners are involved — a man, a woman and God — can we hope to recreate a sense of the seriousness of the obligation undertaken by young people in marriage. In no other way can our generation relearn the truth that marriage is a union of body and spirit, in which husband and wife are bound to each other by a sacred duty which goes far beyond the drive of physical infatuation or the economic and social advantages of living together. We must reject the dangerous and usually insincere doctrine that "love," the physical attraction of two persons, is an all-sufficient condition for marriage and that the absence of compatibility in religious background, education, personal ideals, or temperament is an irrelevant consideration. It is this attitude which leads directly to the idea that any new "affair" into which either partner may permit himself to be drawn may also be justified on the ground of "love," and that the oath of mutual loyalty, which is the heart of the marriage ceremony, may then be abrogated without compunction.

Modern men and women, and above all, contemporary young people, are failing to respond affirmatively to the idea of the holiness of marriage as taught by religion, because they have too often seen it linked with an irrational and unrealistic concept of human nature. Rejecting the latter, they refuse to accept the former. Yet there is no necessary connection between the two. Judaism proves that a rational yet idealistic attitude is entirely possible. Judaism rejects the idea that sex is a sin, marriage a prison, and divorce a punishment for a crime. To fly directly in the face of the realities of human nature means to court disaster. But to accept the natural and to sanctify it, is the heart and essence of the Jewish tradition.

*The three basic, interdependent Jewish concepts of the sanctity of the total human personality, the union of sex and love, and the holiness of marriage offer men and women the greatest measure of hope, as they seek the elusive but eternally beckoning goal of nobler, wiser and happier living.*

# NOTES

1. Quoted in *Time,* January 24, 1964, p. 56. The entire article, "The Second Sexual Revolution" (pp. 54-59), contains valuable data on the contemporary scene.

2. See Lloyd Shearer, "They Had to Get Married" in *Parade,* November 20, 1966, p. 8; see also *Time,* January 27, 1967, p. 76.

3. See *The New York Times,* November 14, 1966.

4. Shearer, *loc. cit.*

5. Cleveland Amory, *The Last Resorts* (New York, 1952).

6. Shearer, *loc. cit.*

7. *Time,* January 24, 1964.

8. I Corinthians 7:1-3, 5-11, 26-28, 36-40 (Revised Standard Version).

9. *The New York Times,* September 21, 1952.

10. See *The New York Times,* December 3, 1966, for a summary of the results of the survey presented to the Fifth Annual Notre Dame Conference on Population by Professor Charles W. Westoff of Princeton University and Professor Norman B. Ryder of the University of Wisconsin.

11. See *The New York Times,* October 29, 1966.

12. See the illuminating studies of Monford Harris: "The Concept of Love in *Sefer Hasidim,*" *Jewish Quarterly Review,* July 1959, pp. 15-44; "The Way of a Man with a Maid — Romantic or Leal Love," *Conservative Judaism,* Winter 1960, pp. 29-39; "Reflections on the Sexual Revolution," *Conservative Judaism,* Spring 1966, pp. 1-17.

13. See for example, A. O. J. Cockshut, *The Unbelievers* (New York, 1966); and see Gertrude Himmelfarb's perspicacious analysis in *New York Review of Books,* November 1, 1966, pp. 20-33.

14. See Robert Gordis, *Judaism in a Christian World* (New York, 1966), esp. pp. 125-180.

15. See Robert Gordis, *Judaism for the Modern Age* (New York, 1955), esp. sec. III, pp. 215-352, for a treatment of several such distinctive aspects of Judaism. Some fundamental divergences in ethical theory between Judaism and Christianity are examined in *idem, The Root and the Branch: Judaism and the Free Society* (Chicago, 1962), chaps. IX-X.

16. The text of *Iggeret Ha-kodesh* is to be found in the excellent edition of Nahmanides' writings by Charles B. Chavel, *Kitvay Rabbenu Moshe ben Nahman* (Jerusalem, 5724-1964), vol. 2, pp. 315-337. The passage we have translated above is in chapter 2 (p. 323). Chavel, who challenges the traditional attribution of the treatise to Nahmanides, was anticipated by Gershom G. Scholem in *Kiryat Sepher,* vol. 25, 1944-45, pp. 179-186. However, as Chavel recognizes, the intrinsic interest of the *Iggeret* is not impugned by the possibility of another author. Nor does Monford Harris' interpretation of the *Iggeret* as possessing an esoteric, kabbalistic meaning (see his paper, "Marriage as Metaphysics — A Study of *Iggeret Hakodesh,*" *Hebrew Union College Annual,* vol. XXXIII, 1962, pp. 197-220) deny its exoteric content as a treatise on love and sex in marriage. Particularly valuable is Harris' explanation of the reason that the author uses the marriage relationship as a vehicle for metaphysical and mystical truth — he thus remains true to Judaism by rejecting the two extremes of libertinism and asceticism, both of which constitute genuine temptations for the devotees of gnosticism, as history demonstrates *(op. cit.,* p. 218 ff.).

17. These Biblical passages are to be found in Deuteronomy 6:5, Leviticus 19:18, and the Song of Songs 7:7, respectively.

18. See the writer's *The Song of Songs* (New York, 1961) *passim.*

19. Tosefta Sanhedrin 12:10.

20. See Mishnah Eduyot 5:3, Tosefta Yadayim 2:14, and the final decision in favor of its canonicity in Mishnah Yadayim 3:5.

21. Midrash Shir Ha-shirim Rabbah on 1:1.

22. B. Berakhot 62a. See the extensive Rabbinic sources on the subject cited in the Bibliography.

23. *Cf.* Bereshit Rabbah, chap. 9; Kohelet Rabbah on Ecclesiastes 3:11; Midrash Tehillim on Psalms 9.

24. *Cf.* B. Berakhot 17a: "Rabbi Alexander, after he prayed, would add, 'O Master of the World, it is revealed and known unto Thee that it is our duty to do Thy will, but what prevents us? The leaven in the dough (*i.e.,* the evil impulse) and the subjection to foreign powers.'"

25. B. Yoma 69b.

26. B. Berakhot 54a.

27. On the theological doctrine of the Fall of Man, which is fundamental to Christian theology, and on the effort to interpret the Biblical view of human nature as evil, see chap. 14, "The Nature of Man in Judaism" in *Judaism for the Modern Age,* cited in note 15.

28. *Cf.* Bereshit Rabbah, chap. 8.

29. *Cf.* Shir Ha-shirim Rabbah, chap. 7.

30. *Cf.* Tosefta Yevamot 8:4; B. Yevamot 63b.

31. B. Avodah Zarah 5b; B. Nedarim 64b.

32. Mishnah Yevamot 6:6; *Shulhan Arukh, Yoreh Deah* 1:5.

33. *Cf. Even Ha-ezer* 23:5 and Rabbi Moses Isserles on 1:3.

34. See Harry Elmer Barnes, "Sex in Education" in V. F. Calverton and S. D. Schmalhausen (eds.), *Sex in Civilization* (New York, 1929), p. 385.

35. For a comprehensive survey of the ideal of *tzeniyut* as applied to modesty in dress and to the segregation of the sexes in Talmudic and post-Talmudic Judaism, see Louis M. Epstein, *Sex Laws and Customs in Judaism* (New York, 1948), pp. 25-103.

36. This is another indication, incidentally, of the literal interpretation of this Biblical book alongside other, more recondite, interpretations.

37. *Cf.* Exodus 21:10; Mishnah Ketubot 5:6; B. Ketubot 61b-62b; *Shulhan Arukh, Even Ha-ezer,* sec. 76.

38. See Rashi on B. Ketubot 62b, *s.v. May'erev Shabbat: Shehu layl ta'anug ushevitah vehana'at ha-guf;* Nahmanides, *Iggeret Ha-kodesh,* sec. 2.

39. *Cf.* B. Yevamot 34b and *Tosafot ad locum;* B. Nedarim 20b and see Isserles on *Even Ha-ezer* 25:2. The classical passage on family limitation occurs in Tosefta Niddah 2:6 with a significant addition, the implications of which are overlooked by Luria and by Lauterbach, whose important paper is cited below. This addition gives considerably greater latitude to irregular forms of sexual play. *Cf. Mitzpeh Shemuel ad locum,* and see also *Yam Shel Shelomoh,* Yevamot 1:8.

40. *Cf.* B. Yevamot 62b.

41. *Ibid.*

42. *Cf.* B. Yevamot 12b, 100b; B. Ketubot 39a; B. Nedarim 35a, 45b; B. Niddah 45a; Tosefta Niddah 2:6; and the lucid and comprehensive study of Jacob Z. Lauterbach, "The Talmudic-Rabbinic View on Birth Control," in the *Central Conference of American Rabbis Year Book,* vol. 37 (1927), pp. 367-384.

43. The Hebrew *meshammeshot bemokh* means lit., "use an absorbent."

44. The remainder of the passage reads as follows: "And who is meant by a 'child wife' *(ketannah)*? From the age of eleven years and a day to twelve and a day. Below this limit and above it, she cohabits in the normal manner, says Rabbi Meir. The Sages say that both within this limit (*i.e.,* from eleven to twelve years), and outside of it (below or above), she cohabits in the normal manner, and Heaven will have pity and protect her, as it is said, 'The Lord guards the simple' (Psalms 116:6)." Thus, regarding the practice of family limitation by the two other categories, there is no disagreement at all in the Talmud. With regard to the first category, the child (from the age of eleven to twelve), Rabbi Meir demands the use of a contraceptive while the Sages trust to Providence to prevent her death from pregnancy. In the ancient Orient, child marriages were fairly common, but were opposed by the Rabbis.

45. The Hebrew participle *meshammeshot* simply means "practice, use." It is given permissive force, "may use," by Rashi (on B. Yevamot 100b), and compulsive force, "must use," by Rab-

benu Jacob Tam (*Tosafot* on B. Ketubot 39a), Asheri, and Rabbenu Nissim (on B. Nedarim 35b). Both interpretations are grammatically sound.

46. *Cf.* Tosefta Yevamot 8:4.

47. Solomon Luria, *Yam Shel Shelomoh,* Yevamot 4:44.

48. *Cf.* Leviticus 18:5 and the interpretation in B. Yoma 85b.

49. See the brief but valuable survey of Immanuel Jakobovits, *Jewish Medical Ethics* (New York, 1959), pp. 167-169, whose treatment of the subject is itself an illustration of this approach.

50. Thus Jakobovits is constrained to admit that "the codes, *rather surprisingly,* omit any direct reference to contraception altogether," *op. cit.,* p. 169 (italics ours). We have indicated above why this approach became dominant in the post-Talmudic era.

51. The literature on the subject is enormous and continually growing. For a brief, balanced statement, see Philip M. Hausner, ed., *The Population Dilemma,* The American Assembly (New York, 1963).

52. For a brief summary of the present situation see the article in *The Wall Street Journal,* December 6, 1966, under the title "Shape of the Future."

53. *Ibid.*

54. The basic prohibition of adultery is, of course, to be found in the Decalogue (Exodus 20:13; Deuteronomy 5:17), the penalty being set forth in Leviticus 20:10.

55. The status of *mamzerut* applies also to the offspring of other forbidden relations, such as incest, the union of close relatives whose marriage to each other is invalid.

56. *Cf.* Mishnah Kiddushin 4:1,2; B. Yevamot 100b. While the second century Mishnaic sage, Rabbi Eliezer, strongly condemns the unmarried woman who has engaged in sexual intimacies (Sifra, *Emor,* chap. 1; B. Yevamot 61b), his views are not shared by the majority of his colleagues. In the medieval period the great Spanish authority, Nahmanides (1194-1270), went so far as to declare that relations with an

unmarried woman, who has no relations with other men, are permissible. This extremely lenient attitude was naturally not accepted universally. Thus, Rabbi Isaac bar Sheshet Perfet (1326-1408), who cites Nahmanides' view (*Responsa* 6,398), was far stricter. While he decried the popular saying *pelonit penuyah muteret,* he saw other and greater threats to traditional standards of personal morality in his time (*Responsum* 425; see also no. 6 and no. 395 on concubinage). *Cf.* Abraham M. Hershman, *Rabbi Isaac bar Sheshet Perfet and His Times* (New York, 1943), esp. pp. 143-145, and Yitzhak Baer, *A History of the Jews in Christian Spain,* vol. II (Philadelphia, 1966), pp. 465-466.

57. *Cf.* the statement in J. Pesahim 10:1, p. 37b (Venice ed.): "Rabbi Levi said, 'He who eats *matzah* on the eve of Passover (*i.e.,* before the advent of the Festival) is like a man who has relations with his betrothed in the house of his father-in-law (*i.e.,* before marriage). He who is guilty of this offense (*i.e.,* the eating of *matzah*) is punished by flagellation.'" See also Rambam, *Mishneh Torah, Hilkhot Hametz Umatzah* 6:12. Note the insight into human frailty underlying the analogy between the two acts, coupled with the negative judgment involved in the penalty that is indicated in the Talmud and the Codes.

58. According to the Codes, intimate relations by engaged couples are prohibited not Biblically but only Rabbinically (*Mishneh Torah, Hilkhot Ishut* 10:1; *Tur, Even Ha-ezer* 55:1). The Talmud and the Geonim declare that there was substantial freedom in the relations of engaged couples in the period ot Ezra and Nehemiah. Thus they interpret *benay tabaot* (in Nehemiah 7:46) as the offspring of pre-nuptial unions; *cf. Otzar Ha-geonim, Kiddushin,* sec. 23, p. 187. In Tannaitic times, private companionship for couples before marriage was permitted in Judea, though not in Galilee (Mishnah Ketubot 1:5; Tosefta Ketubot 1:4; B. Ketubot 12a). The stricter Galilean rule became the norm in Talmudic and post-Talmudic law. See *Enzyklopediah Talmudit* (Jerusalem, 1949), vol. 2, p. 182b, for a compendium of the sources and Louis M. Epstein,

*op. cit.,* p. 126. Undoubtedly the practice was less rigorous than the legal standard. See the preceding note for analogies.

59. See *The New York Times,* October 15, 1966: "No rule can cover all the varied and complex situations in which men and women find themselves," the report asserts. "Moreover, an action which is in outward conformity with a rule may nonetheless be immoral because the motive and spirit behind it are wrong." The Rev. Kenneth G. Greet, a Methodist who was chairman of the commission working on the report, explained that there had been a "deliberate refusal to do what many Christian people would want us to do." He said he hoped the report would do something to help correct the "distorted image" of the church as consisting of "sexless saints sitting in judgment on the passionate sins of less disciplined mortals. . . . Apart from the lingering risk of unwanted children, intercourse is so significant that it cannot be separated from love and long-term commitment, without the partners, and society, suffering some harm." This principle, he says, is "not quite" the same thing as the old rule.

60. *Cf.* B. Gittin 90b.

61. *Cf.* Moses Mielziner, *Jewish Law of Marriage and Divorce,* 2nd ed. (New York, 1901); Louis M. Epstein, *The Jewish Marriage Contract* (New York, 1927); and *Marriage Laws in the Bible and Talmud* (Cambridge, 1942); Boaz Cohen, *Law and Tradition in Judaism* (New York, 1959), chap. V, "Concerning the Jewish Law of Domestic Relations," pp. 100-118. For a recent consideration of this mounting problem, see *Proceedings of Conference on Divorce in the Jewish Community,* October 19-20, 1966, published by the Federation of Jewish Philanthropies of New York.

62. A reasoned plea for recognizing that divorce may be the preferable alternative to an unhappy marriage is made in Morton M. Hunt's book, *The World of the Formerly Married* (New York, 1966). His views are summarized in his article, "Help Wanted: Divorce Counselor" in *The New York Times Magazine,* January 1, 1967, pp. 14-17. He maintains that this approach is making relatively slow progress because "one

does not argue about such things; what is right is right and what is wrong is wrong, because it has always been so and because everyone knows it to be so." The true reason inheres in the New Testament teaching forbidding divorce, which has survived in theory even when it has been abandoned in practice.

63. The sociologist F. Nye Nye found more delinquent behavior, poorer adjustment to parents and more psychosomatic ailments among a large group of adolescents from intact unhappy homes than among the offspring of broken homes. Dr. Lee Burchinall found no significant differences in the emotional health of grade school students from intact homes (happy or unhappy) and that of children whose parents had been divorced. See the article by Morton M. Hunt cited in note 62.

64. Mishnah Gittin 9:5.

65. For the history of this painful problem, see A. H. Freimann, *Seder Kiddushin Unesu'in* (Jerusalem, 5705-1945); I. Z. Kahana, *Sefer Ha-agunot* (Jerusalem, 5714-1954) and Louis M. Epstein, *Lishe'elat Ha-agunah* (New York, 5700-1940). Epstein's proposal, made earlier, for dealing with the problem was officially adopted by the Rabbinical Assembly in 1935 but was not implemented. The Assembly subsequently adopted the enlarged version of the *Ketubah* sponsored by Professor Saul Lieberman.

# BIBLIOGRAPHY

## A. BIBLICAL SOURCES

Genesis — chaps. 1, 2, 16, 18
Exodus — chap. 21
Leviticus — chaps. 18, 20
Deuteronomy — chaps. 21, 22
Psalms — chaps. 127, 128, 133
Song of Songs

## B. RABBINIC SOURCES

*The Mishnah* (trans. by Herbert Danby), 3rd sec., *Nashim* ("Women"), pp. 217-230

The Babylonian Talmud, Section *Nashim*

Rabbi Moses ben Maimon, *Mishneh Torah, Hilkhot Ishut*

Rabbi Joseph Karo, *Shulhan Arukh, Even Ha-ezer*

## C. MODERN STUDIES

Bailey, D. S., *Sexual Relation and Christian Thought* (New York, 1959)

Doniger, S., ed., *Sex and Religion* (New York, 1953)

Epstein, Louis M., *The Jewish Marriage Contract* (New York, 1927)

——*Marriage Laws in the Bible and the Talmud* (Cambridge, 1942)

——*Sex Laws and Customs in Judaism* (New York, 1948)

——*Lishe'elat Ha-agunah* (New York, 5700-1940)

Freimann, A. H., *Seder Kiddushin Unesu'in* (Jerusalem, 5705-1945)

Gittelsohn, Roland, *Consecrated Unto Me* (New York, 1965)

Goldstein, Sidney E. *The Meaning of Marriage and Foundations of the Family* (New York, 1940)

Gordis, Robert, *Judaism for the Modern Age* (New York, 1955)

——*The Root and the Branch: Judaism and the Free Society* (Chicago, 1962)

Hardin, Garrett, ed., *Population, Evolution, Birth Control* (San Francisco, London, 1964)

Hausner, Philip M., ed., *The Population Dilemma,* The American Assembly (New York, 1963)

Jakobovits, Immanuel, *Jewish Medical Ethics* (New York, 1959)

Kahana, I. Z., *Sefer Ha-agunot* (Jerusalem, 5714-1954)

Mielziner, Moses, *Jewish Law of Marriage and Divorce* (New York, 1901)

*Proceedings of Conference on Divorce in the Jewish Community,* October 19-20, 1966, sponsored by Federation of Jewish Philanthropies of New York

*Proceedings of Conference on Intermarriage and the Future of the American Jew,* December 1964, sponsored by Commission on Synagogue Relations, Federation of Jewish Philanthropies of New York

Rabinowitz, Stanley, *A Jewish View of Love and Marriage* (Washington, D. C., 1961)

*Sex and the College Student,* Group for the Advancement of Psychiatry, Report #60 (New York, 1965)

Sussman, Marvin B., ed., *Sourcebook on Marriage and the Family,* 2nd ed. (Boston, 1963)

# INDEX

60